To My Son,
Twelve Lessons I've Learned
Father and Son Connected Forever

Your Father
Jimmy E. McMillian

To My Son, Twelve Lessons I've Learned, Father and Son Connected Forever
ISBN 978-0-9847742-5-8
Copyright © 2016 Jimmy E. McMillian

Request for information should be addressed to:
Curry Brothers Marketing and Publishing Group
P.O. Box 247
Haymarket, VA 20168

All rights reserved. No part of this publication may be reproduced, stored in a retrieval system, or transmitted in any form or by any means, electronic, mechanical, photocopy, recording, or any other, except for brief quotations in printed reviews, without the prior permission of the publisher.

HOPE

Hope is not blind optimism. It's not ignoring the enormity of the task ahead or the roadblocks that stand in our path. It's not sitting on the sidelines or shirking from a fight. Hope is that thing inside us that insists, despite all evidence to the contrary, that something better awaits us if we have the courage to reach for it, and to fight for it. Hope is the belief that destiny will not be written for us, but by us, by the men and women who are not content to settle for the world as it is, who have the courage to remake the world as it should be.

— Barack Obama

"Therefore you shall be careful to do as the Lord your God has commanded you; you shall not turn aside to the right hand or to the left."

Deuteronomy 5:32

Introduction

"It is easier to raise strong children than to repair broken men"

Fredrick Douglass

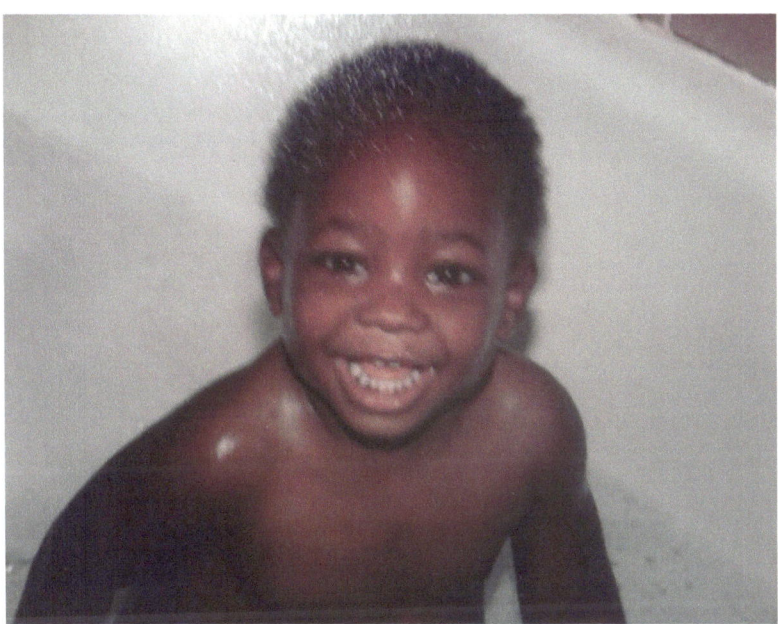

Darrius,

I want you to know how much I admire the young man you have become and the future I envision for you. You are the pride of our family and the reason your mother and I have endured the sacrifices of investing our souls in you. Our hearts are filled with more joy, and love than we have time to express. My intent in writing this is to share with you some of the lessons I learned from the highs and lows I endured in my life, where I turned for strength during my time of weaknesses and how I avoided the pitfalls designed to kill me.

I vividly recall the first time our eyes connected, the first time you squeezed my finger and when I took you on our first walk hand-in-hand. I can still hear your toddler laugh that makes me wish for our time past. Through you, I learned the true essence of a father and son connection, although I never had a father to call my own. Fatherhood teaches you that responsibility is required, commitment is sacred, love is plentiful, and time is valuable.

As you mature never forget that responsibility for your actions cannot be transferred to others. You must always own whatever mess you make and be the one to clean it up. Allowing unresolved situations to linger complicates your life and impedes your future success. Never expect to succeed if you do not take the initiative to prepare for opportunities presented unexpectedly. No one owes you anything but if you have a reputation for diligence and are responsible, people will remember the goodness of your name and the work of your hands and mind. Be steadfast and committed in all that is worth doing for the improvement of life and human kind.

Commitment is sacred and when you commit to someone or something, always follow through and stay in the trenches until commitments are fulfilled. When you fail in your commitments you lose credibility and trustworthiness; you disappoint people and especially the people that love you. If you neglect to care and love the family you create your reputation as a father and a man is tarnished and it is difficult to reboot whatever respect you once enjoyed. Do what you love and commitment is easy.

As my son you opened doors in my heart I never knew existed, or realized how tightly they were closed. I released my stored protected love to you because I now know it was missing in my childhood and realized how important it is to have a father that displays love and caring for his son. The greatest display of love is when it is demonstrated in all things great and small, even if you do not receive it in return. When you become a father always love your children and spouse in both good and bad times. I did not always live up to this standard and regret the times I failed to love you and your mother as you both deserved. I remember when I first told you I loved you but you were not old enough to respond in words.

But your immediate hug help me understand that love resonates in all of us regardless of age. Always look your family in the eyes as often as possible and tell them they are loved by you forever. Love is measured in our actions and responses to family situations. How you as the man, father and husband responds to family dynamics will certainly determine the outcomes. Stay under control and when you are emotional, remove yourself from the scene and pray for guidance rather than "rely on your own understanding." Time can heal most situations but it requires a tremendous amount of patience for a favorable resolution. I did not always model this behavior for you but it is a lesson I learned.

Time goes fast, and now that you are graduating from your undergraduate curriculum validates time is a precious commodity when spent with the people we love. There were times when I was too busy to listen to you, too tired to play with you and too far away to embrace you—please forgive me. I want you to understand there is nothing more rewarding than time spent between father and son. Whatever occupation you select to earn a living always make a life with your family the priority. When your children or spouse need you, be there no matter what, put their time on your calendar just as you do important business meetings, accompany your children to as many of their events as possible even when you are tired and sleepy. I took a nap at many of our Disney World movies but I was present. I attended 90 percent of your football games, martial arts competitions, piano recitals, soccer games, track meets and youth basketball games. After long hours at work I read all your favorite books to you, and you chastised me if I skipped pages to expedite the time. That time will always be valuable, and the memories of our time together are forever etched in my heart as the corner stone of my life, and it is an eternal blessing to me to have a son of your caliber.

Love Always,

Dad

Also I heard the voice of the Lord, saying; who shall I send, and who will go for us? Then I said, "Here am I, send me."

Isaiah 6:8

Lesson # 1

Make God, Prayer and Faith First in Your Life

Expect to have difficulty navigating your way through this maze we call life. Expect to fail even after giving it your best. Expect temptations crafted by evil doers to lure you into a false sense of serenity. When these devices are weighing heavy in your life resort to my "dusty knee concept" and cry out to the God we taught you to serve from the depths of your soul. Pray with earnest and he will answer your call. He will enter and release you from the shackles of disappointment, ill-repute, and any fears that impede your divine greatness.

Do not be dismayed by your trials and tribulation when God's grace is available to sustain you and usher you through the insurmountable odds stacked against you. Be faithful and believe in your prayers while in the fray and expect to be delivered from the evil. Faith is a powerful weapon only if you operate in its sphere. Faith requires a tremendous amount of work when you arise from your knees. After earnest prayer, you must stand with a belief not disturbed by any of life's circumstance. Your grandmother, Mary defined the elegance of faith. She invested in me even when my future appeared bleak. She loaned me money to finish my last semester while your mother and I were dating. She stepped out on faith and her only request was I never quit on my education. I repaid her but her faith taught me to pass God's blessings on. Mayo Angelo's poem "she is a phenomenal woman and should make all women proud to spell their name…WOMAN" is the best description of your grandmother, not to mention her purity and virtuous life style everyone admired.

You will always be confronted with a choice between right and wrong. I did not always do the right thing. Trying to do the right thing is difficult but it is more challenging to live with your conscious if you fail to do whatever is right. Never allow others to steal your faith, stay true to what God has promised and walk confident toward your divine purpose even when you have to do it alone.

The old people in my community use to say "stayed prayed up because you never know what is lurking just up the road." I pray all the time regardless of where I am or what I'm doing. You do not have to be in a place of worship, you do not have to be among fellow Christians, it does not have to be in a quiet place, but it must be sincere and God will hear you. It was prayer, faith, grace and mercy that delivered me to this place and time of my life. I was confronted with temptations but mustered the will to overcome by the grace of God. When evil ejected me to the ground I landed in the arms of God and that is where I gained the strength to slay my demons one by one and he will do the same for you. Prayer, faith and God will get you through all tribulations, but you have to glorify him with all the credit.

My Dad's promotion to General Officer; Hard work, Discipline, Faith and Prayer makes a difference.

Lesson # 2
Discipline and Determination Makes the Difference

Son, without focused discipline and an uncompromising determination life will ignore all your attempts to succeed. Remember, no one owes you anything and there will always be someone trying to take what you earned. Never surrender to negative thinking, never associate with naysayers, surround yourself with people who are where you desire to ascend. Always possess the discipline to reject anything or anyone that interferes or distracts you from achieving your God given goals. Remain disciplined enough to be alone and unafraid, but driven to succeed without compromising your ethics or morality. You may not be the smartest person in the room but your discipline and determination will be sufficient to remain equal because no one will ever out work you. Always be willing to die trying because there is no joy in self-defeat.

The successful people I know have several things in common, 1) they are resilient, disciplined and focus on the task at hand; 2) they align themselves with people who share their passion and they are not disillusioned by temporary set-backs; 3) their work ethic is unmatched and they seek opportunities to improve their professions; and 4) they never waste time with trivial matters that drain energy.

Discipline and determination are paramount to beating the odds, and overcoming the obstacles that hinders progress. The most challenging situations are conquered by the determination to see it through and the discipline to eliminate tentative efforts. William Faulkner said, "do not bother to be better than your contemporaries or predecessors. Try to be better than yourself." The only person that can limit your success is you, but self-discipline and determination can preclude such an outcome.

I know there were times in our home when you felt my discipline was merciless and I was often criticized by other parents for such strict discipline, not abuse. The children of those parents are confused, aimlessly wandering looking for direction, searching for validation, disobedient to the very parents that nursed their lives.

Your mother was criticized for teaching you to read at age three and I pushed you relentlessly to achieve nothing but academic excellence. When you were a toddler and your mother was not physically available to read to you, she recorded her voice reading your favorite books to you on an antiquated tape recorder. We taught you how to answer the phone appropriately, we demanded you say yes sir and no sir, yes ma'am and no ma'am, everyone complimented the firmness of your handshake at age 8 and marveled at your eye contact when conversing with others. We selected books for you to read during the summer breaks and you prepared book reports to validate your understanding of the readings, your mother assigned you homework in the summer to prepare you for the next academic year. We developed spelling test to aid you in achieving A's on all your spelling test in 1st through the 4th grade. You had room inspections to appreciate structure and cleanliness. I exposed you to physical fitness and healthy eating; you never saw your father and mother drunk and despicable. I'm not suggesting we were perfect parents in anyway, but through it all our primary focus was setting you up for success. All of these efforts were instrumental in shaping what you have accomplished up to this point in your life…you make me proud to call you my son!

You are not in jail, you are not on drugs, you do not have anyone pregnant, you do not smoke cigarettes, you do not indulge in alcohol; you have a

My parents who made me a man!

respectful grade point average in a challenging area of study, and you respect adults regardless of their economic status. The world awaits you and your legacy has just begun. Run the good race!

Darrius high school track, running the race for life.

"I have been crucified with Christ and I no longer live, but Christ lives in me. The life I now live in the body, I live by faith in the Son of God, who loved me and gave himself for me."

Galatians 2:20

Lesson # 3

Continual Learning Enriches Your Life

Always look for opportunities to educate yourself because if you are not learning you are dying. Dr. Martin Luther King, Jr. advocated that, "Our lives begin to end the day we become silent about things that matter." Continual learning matters. Education is one of the best passports to succeeding in life and cannot be taken from you once you have it. Education is more than achieving a college degree or having superior intellect. Paraphrasing Mark Twain, intellect without wisdom or morality is no intellect at all. Cultivate an insatiable appetite for learning to propel you beyond human limitations. Read about people who have conquered seemingly impossible challenges and left a legacy that transcends time. Visit places to learn different cultures but be endowed in your own history before you embark on another history.

Dedicate some time to read every day beyond the office or the lecture hall. In quiet spaces we meet ourselves and examine the depths of our souls that will stir emotion to act for the betterment of mankind. Learning is constant but you must have an open mind to benefit from the teachings of others or your surroundings, both good and bad. A man with the desire to improve his life must have the capacity and will to remain a constant student of learning. Every three years you should be in some school or institution preparing to learn something new, or teaching those that can share their knowledge with you.

On the grounds of the United States Air Force Academy, there is a quote that reads a "man's flight through life is sustained by the power of his knowledge." Without knowledge you cannot advance your cause, you will not realize your purpose or have the mental acuity to develop your vision. And without a vision you will perish and become irrelevant. Keep learning to remain relevant and productive.

I was inspired to get an education because of the conditions I endured as child. If you expected to live in comfort during this life education is a necessity. My mother did not have any idea on how to help me obtain an education, but she knew it was important as evidenced by her constant reminder to maintain good grades and stay in school. It was always perplexing to me how she recognized the value of an education but never found the spark to ignite the flame to obtain such for herself. I used my love for reading and writing poetry to escape my conditions and emotionally disconnect from the hardships of a single parent home.

Through books I encountered great people making a difference and turning tragedy into triumph. Reading provided me insights into the lives of other people and forced me to mentally travel to places that I could never afford to visit. While reading was my refuge from shame and despair of poverty it generated confidence in me no one could take away or undermine. I promised myself that I would get an education and never quit no matter how long it took to obtain.

Therefore, I expect you to possess the same dedication and follow the example illustrated by your mother and me. The living conditions I inherited at birth energized me to follow God's pre-ordained steps to my destiny. I always believed there was a better way to live the true essence of one's life rather than accept the life created by human failures.

Your successful completion of high school and college has cemented the template for learning in your DNA. It does not take much effort to recognize the plight of people that did not find the determination to pursue education, or understand the long term implications of a life without a sufficient education to live, not just exist. Education can balance the playing field when the odds are not in your favor. The pursuit of constant learning positions you to challenge the establishment with confidence and create a history of significance for your family, and your race. Russian Vice Admiral Kotenlnikov said "Keep learning to keep winning, if you stop learning, you stop creating history and become history." Your ancestors are depending on you to create more history.

Left to right: Dad, Great grandmother Sophia (103YOA), Grandmother Novella; in the rear Aunt Alberta and Aunt Martha.

"And Bezalel and Aholiab, and every gifted artisan in whom the Lord has put wisdom and understanding, to know how to do all manner of work for the service of the sanctuary, shall do according to all that the Lord has commanded."

Exodus 36:1

THE FIRST SEMESTER
By Dr. Boyce Watkins

Listen up people, you can all now relax
Einstein has arrived, and you can ride on my back
Oh you ain't heard? I'm a genius you see
These scrubs pay tuition, but I attend school for free
If you think that I'm joking, then please have no doubt
I got more awards in high school than the Grammies give out
They call you the fraction, I's 100 percent
If brains were like money, I'm the national mint
Profs say that I'm tripping, but I'll make them say "wow"
Why don't you just give me my straight As right now?
Cause you know it's a forgone when it comes to the books
Just call me the dial tone cause I'm straight off the hook
Now I'm on campus, but I must split my time
Cause the opposite sex is just looking so fine
My old friends from high school? I ain't stuttin them geeks
Cause I was just asked to be one of the greeks
I took over this campus right out of the box
Me and my homies got the parties on lock
When I go to the club, they call me the fish
Cause I drink like a guppie inside a dish
I know that you're worried, but don't be alarmed
I keep busy, but you know that my grades won't be harmed
Oh, about that math test? Don't worry bout it cuz
Alright….Ok, what had happened wuz…..
Imma be real, I won't tell you no lies
My midterms had grades that I don't recognize
But that's all gonna change cause I'm more focused see
I'll be studying with Billy, Tyrone, Angie and T
They say that studying in groups doesn't work all that well
I told Dr. Watkins, and he just said "Awwwww hayell"

He said I was getting too carried away
And in the long run, there's a price I would pay
How does that little cricket know what life's all about?
No He needs to just keep my name out his mouth
I'm not his son, his daughter, his husband or wife
How can that fool know what's best for MY LIFE?
My report card should be arriving today
My grades are not perfect, but they should be ok
I procrastinated a little, I must confess
But I DID study all night before I took the test
I open the mailbox with real shaky hands
My parents are sweating me like internal glands
I creak open the paper, then a little more
The first letter makes my mother pass out on the floor
I now get a seizure like epilepsy
Cause my report card is yelling "FDDFC!"
Daddy is about to have cardiac arrest
If his cussin were holy, I would have been SUPER BLESSED
My face fills with liquid from all of my tears
Cleaning this mess will take 2 or 3 years
My friends that studied and partied with me
Are back home with their mama's just watching TV
It was bad enough hearing my parents lip
But the school is now taking my whole scholarship
If my brain were really the national mint
I would have looked at the scholarship and all the fine print
College is thunder, you already know
But if I could start over, I would have started off slow
Cause things don't always go as we planned
There's a whole lot of distraction in this wonderland
Have fun while in college, but don't lose your mind
Smart students have BALANCE and get on the grind
Be smart with your choices, don't forget who you be
Or you'll be home with yo mama, just hanging with me!

Lesson # 4

Live Your Life to Inspire People Not to Impress People

If you desire to inspire people, always reflect your divine image and not your man made facade. Set your sights on what is right and embrace justice, and not for what is popular or convenient. Never settle for mere acceptance in the fraternity of stagnation, greed, and institutional bias. Challenge yourself to rise above the ego that prevents you from reaching to others requesting a hand-up not a hand-out. You should never walk past the lonely without a spoken word of encouragement.

Someone penned these words "encouraged people achieve best; dominated people achieve second best; neglected people achieve the least." In the words of William Arthur, "flatter me, and I may not believe you. Criticize me, and I may not like you. Ignore me, and I may not forgive you. Encourage me, and I may not forget you". Son, these quotes were sent to me from a friend when I rendered an act of kindness at a special time in their lives. Always arouse people to raise their thinking beyond institutional or self-imposed limitations.

I employ you to treat everyone with dignity even when you are justified by their actions to retaliate with force. Always set the conditions for decency, transparency and truth in your dealings with people. Keep your integrity at the core of your being to drive your character. Once your integrity is stripped from you, it is difficult to reclaim. Integrity is the armor that protects you from decadences of a corrupt world. Look for the best in people and compliment those who are steadfast in doing the right thing.

Never expect anything in return for the good you do to help your community, a fellow-man, or institution. Be content when confronting controversy, and while fighting for people without a voice. The deserving voiceless will be forever grateful for your commitment to them. Remain true to yourself and develop a character of courage that surpasses small minds.

During your journey you will meet people that are selfish, untrustworthy, filled with material wealth, and possess the political and personal connections that reads like a list "Who's who" in the world. I demand that you judge people by the size of their heart not the size of their financial portfolio or to whom they are connected. Richness is not measured in dollars and cents, but rather in service and wisdom. The best days of my life was having someone say I inspired them to be their best, motivated them to change a bad behavior or move their life in a positive direction. As I have always conveyed to you in words and action, it is never what we do for ourselves that matter most, but what we do for others deserving of our time and resources.

Inspiration comes from within and your presence should stimulate people to be better than the best. Although you will never be God, but if you live according to his purpose everyone will recognize there is something different about you. People will become magnetized by the God in you without knowing why. Make the time to inspire people beyond their own comprehension and never accept gratitude for their success. If they want to repay you ask them to pay it forward to a deserving person that will ultimately inspire others as you did them.

Darrius high school football running back—no obstacle too difficult.

"I can do all things through Christ who strengthens me"
Philippians 4:13

"So Joshua conquered all the land: the mountain country and the South and the lowland and the wilderness slopes, and all their kings; he left none remaining, but utterly destroyed all that breathed, as the Lord God of Israel had commanded."

Joshua 10:40

Lesson # 5

Trust is Sacred be Careful Where You Deposit It

"Love all, trust few."

William Shakespeare

Trust and respect is earned and never for sale to the highest bidder with the most wealth or prestige. It is vital that you exercise extreme caution before you extend your precious trust to others. There are people standing in line to rob you of your trust and misuse it for selfish gain. Son, remember, "God gives wisdom to the wise, and knowledge to the discerning." Daniel 2:21. People will deceive you when you are most vulnerable and betray your trust; they will embrace you tightly and wipe your tears from a broken situation and stab you in the back at the same time. It is only the people who are closest to you that can break you. Judge your associates with strict criteria and prove them worthy of your trust before you welcome them in your life.

There are people endowed with hate, jealousy, and professional envy. They will bait you and then seek to destroy the very life you have constructed for your well-being. Do not be fooled by good looks, charisma, money, material wealth or prestigious occupations. Backstabber's, haters and fictitious people come in all disguises masquerading to defraud your livelihood, not to enhance you. As I have reminded you on several occasions, if people are not adding to your life they are taking from your life. The worst part of this scenario is that you may never recognize the scheme until it is too late, therefore pray for the spirit of discernment when dealing with people.

In a lifetime if you are fortunate enough, you may meet more than three people you can call friend outside your immediate family and future bride. It takes years to develop a genuine friendship with a trustworthy person. I want you to always be friendly but do not expect to gain a friend. True friends are always in your court even when you cannot help them, they will not abandon you when you are in trouble, they will

stand with you when the seas are raging in your life and the winds are disturbing the progress in your life. More importantly they will love you when you make a mistake and not criticize you later.

Trust your God more than you trust anything or anyone else and you will never be disappointed. I have always been a loner although I know many people. I find solace in being alone in most situations because it allows me to reflect and think without interruptions and I find most people do not share my beliefs or values. I have very few people I call friend and the ones I call friend have been with me for years. I trust them with all my possessions. I was blessed to make some great friends and so will you. I'm certain my friends have helped me in so many ways. They are Chaplain Keith & Debbie Darlington, Col Henry & Teresa Mitnaul, Dr. Col Gerald & Gloria Curry, Lt Col Wally & Ginger Pope, Dr. Olenda Johnson, Col Emmitt Mitchell, Robert McAllister, Cynthia Wells, and John Fedrigo. These are my friends besides you, God and your mother. I have known some of these people for thirty years and one person all my life. The message for you is it takes time to build meaningful friendships, and only extend your trust to people who will not compromise it, but to only those that will protect it and honor it.

Left to right; Darrius, BG McMillian (Dad), Col Mitnaul, and Col (Chaplin) Darlington (Friends for Life)

Col (Dr.) Gerald Curry and Dad

From left to right: Darrius, Mary, Debbie, Teresa, Jocelyne, Dr. Johnson, Col Mitnaul, Deborah, Col (Chaplin) Darlington (Sincere Friends)

Cynthia "CJ" Wells

John Fedrigo
Served as my Deputy Director of Security Forces,
Headquarters, U.S. Air Force

Lesson # 6

You are Always on Parade

The world only observes what is good and what is not good and responds either negatively or positively. Unfortunately, as a Black Man you will experience harsh criticisms publically, and privately regardless of your preparation, education, or perspiration from hard work. More than your best will be demanded of you by the world and you owe it to your ancestors that made the ultimate sacrifice for you to be the best. I'm not indicating the entire world is unjust and racist, but do not expect it to extend an olive branch to you. I have experienced bigotry from all races. The most difficult bigotry to endure is from the people that look like you. But do not be discouraged by their ignorance, being your best in all things will overcome ignorance. The image you present is the first thing people will notice, and as the saying goes "you only get one chance to make a good first impression."

From this time forward what you do is no longer about you, but about the people you represent, such as your parents, your forbearers, and younger people desiring to be like you. Present yourself in a dignified manner, be appropriately dressed for all occasions, and speak intelligently at all times, remain confident and self-respecting. Everyone respects what they admire even if they never say it to you. Be the model for all just like President Obama, even if in the face of ill content.

Make excellence your hallmark and outstanding your way of life. Every endeavor you pursue and every product you produce must be excellent, there is no substitute for a standard of excellence. It must resonate in your home and your work, in your relationships, in your academics, in your preparations and in your service to others. Never settle for anything less than the best because once you compromise your standard of excellence, life will never be what you deserve and society will remember you as a failure.

As your parade moves through life I personally believe you must strive for perfection. There are some who will disagree with the premise that perfection is unattainable, but what I know for sure, if you are not striving for perfection the standard of excellence and outstanding will allude you forever. Perfection is attainable! The world is watching you every day and it may not matter what the world thinks of you, but you have an obligation to leave a lasting impression of excellence everywhere you go and in everything you do.

Dad's Honorary Chief's Ceremony. Darrius coined for being a great son

Lesson # 7

Manage your Finances

There will come a day when you will not be able to work or retired from an occupation. There is a saying "a penny saved is a penny earned" and it all adds up to dollars. Everyone must have a savings to realize the "American Dream." Our dreams are often deferred because we mismanage our finances and neglect to save or invest in our future and the future of our families. I encouraged you to save and invest at least 10 percent of your income with 15 percent as the goal. Invest according to your risk tolerance and become intelligent on how the financial world operates.

I have learned you must have some money saved for unforeseen contingencies and be in a position to afford the great opportunities life has to offer. Do not waste money on things that do not matter or things you cannot afford. Never spend money just to impress your professional acquaintances. Your mother and I kept our personal vehicles an average of 15 years but we had enough funds to purchase our first home by age 30. And given from where we started that is a remarkable blessing.

Credit cards without spending discipline is a recipe for financial disaster or ruin. My advice is to avoid them early on in your career and if you must use a credit card have sufficient funding to pay the balance in full at each billing cycle. The interest rates are generally too high and normally there is nothing you need immediately that cannot wait until you save to purchase it. Delayed gratification is a wise concept in the world of financial responsibility. I waited 30 years before I purchased the personal vehicle of my dreams. Each time I was tempted to purchase the wrist watch of my dreams I delayed it to have funding for more important financial obligations, such as your first car after college, your college tuition, the braces for your teeth, your music and martial arts lessons, your clothing, your food, your shelter and our family vacations when possible. Money will not make you complete but if you spend it on what truly matters it will add value to the quality of life.

Do not loan money to family and some friends. It is prudent to just gift it to them because in most instances they will never pay you back. When you lend money to people and they do not repay as agreed you will lose respect for them over time and it will strain the relationship. If you can afford to help someone with your finances then I employ you to so. But do not give repeatedly to the same people if you do not receive a good return on your investment. A lasting return is when the borrower summons the will to alleviate whatever is detracting from their financial well-being. If someone refuses to change their financial situation with your financial assistance you are contributing to a bad situation, setting them up for constant failure.

Please do not allow money to rule your thinking, never hoard it for evil or selfish gain, do not waste it on foolishness. Consider contributing to charities of your choice to make a difference. Consult a financial advisor with integrity to assist you in planning your financial portfolio for the grey hair years if necessary. A balanced approach to managing your finances will leave generational wealth and improve the lives of those you love, it is a responsibility you cannot afford to ignore.

"Though the colored man is no longer subject to barter and sale, he is surrounded by an adverse settlement which fetters all his movements. In his downward course he meets with no resistance, but his course upward is resented and resisted at every step of his progress. If he comes in ignorance, rags and wretchedness he conforms to the popular belief of his character, and in that character he is welcome; but if he shall come as a gentleman, a scholar and statesman, he is hailed as a contradiction to the national faith concerning his race, and his coming is presented as impudence. In one case, he may provoke contempt derision, but in the other he is an affront to pride and provokes malice."

Frederick Douglass

Lesson #8

Take Care of Your Health

A man is no good to himself, his family, his community or his God in self-induced poor health. None of us know what is lurking in our bodies as a result of our genetic make-up but we all know what constitutes great physical, emotional and spiritual health. There is nothing more important than being in great physical health augmented by emotional and spiritual health. If you expect to realize your divine purpose your health will be paramount through that journey. There will always be impediments to obtaining great health in the triad of the physical, emotional and spiritual arenas. You must find that focused discipline I discussed earlier to remove obstacles that hinder your commitment to this important aspect of your life.

Physical Health

Regardless of your occupation, the hours you work, demanding family commitments, and community obligations, you owe it to yourself to carve out the time to take care of your physical fitness. The benefits are life lasting—you feel better, you look better, you are more confident in your abilities, people will respect your discipline and you have the energy to endure the demands in your life. Spend at least four days a week meeting your physical fitness goals. Do not allow your friends, your dates with the significant other, your spouse, your studies to interfere with your physical fitness standards. At the end of the day if your health fails then you are no good to anything or anybody. You will have to sacrifice to make it a priority even if it means getting up early to get it done.

Solid as a rock

Langley bodybuilder wins major title

By Steve Hanf
Staff writer

Leaders have traditionally been strong men, but few have ever been this strong.

Maj. Jim McMillian, an Air Combat Command Inspector General security police section chief, has been a bodybuilder since he joined the Air Force 13 years ago. McMillian said the disciplines of bodybuilding and the Air Force have gone hand-in-hand.

"As an officer and a leader, I ought to set an example," McMillian said. "When I'm in uniform I want people to say, 'Is that the Air Force standard?'"

McMillian said he has always liked structure and discipline, which he found in bodybuilding and the Air Force. He decided long ago that he would live by the creed of, "A healthy body promotes a healthy mind."

He said that at the age of 11 he decided he would not drink alcohol or smoke cigarettes and that he would get the proper rest he needed. The walls in his room were decorated with posters from muscle magazines, and he decided that he wanted to look like those men some day.

McMillian has looked ready for a fitness magazine this year, winning five of the six competitions he has entered. His most recent victory was the 35- to 39-year-old master's division Mr. Virginia title May 6 at the Amateur Athletic Union Virginia State Bodybuilding Competition in Hampton.

The May 6 competition was the biggest contest McMillian had ever won he said. The victory did not come without some sacrifices, though.

"The diet was the toughest part," McMillian said. "But there was also a loss in family time."

McMillian had to go from his usual 205-pound, eight percent body fat frame into contest shape.

A1C William Greer

Maj. Jim McMillian, an Air Combat Command Inspector General security police section chief, poses at the Amateur Athletic Union Virginia State Bodybuilding Competition held in Hampton May 6. McMillian won the master's division Mr. Virginia title.

He peaks at contests at around 180 pounds and three percent to five percent body fat.

McMillian uses a disciplined workout regimen to keep himself in peak form. He appears at the gym at 5 a.m. four to five days a week for an hour-and-a-half workout. His contest training schedule increases his workouts to two-a-day three times a week and single workouts twice a week.

"If I'm going to train, I train my very best," McMillian said. "I'm not training for second place."

One of the key elements to McMillian's training is aerobic workouts. He always does 30 minutes of aerobic exercise to get his body warmed up, and says aerobics helps the cardiovascular system. McMillian said the aerobic element to his training is one of the key differences between himself and other bodybuilders in the gym.

"Other lifters are hung-up on the amount of weight that they're lifting," McMillian said. "But you're intensity level and diet are the most important things involved."

Which is not to say that McMillian cannot lift with the best of them. His personal best is a 505-pound squat, "all the way up and all the way down, like it's supposed to be done," McMillian added.

Another difference between McMillian and other bodybuilders is diet.

"If you leave the gym and go to Burger King or McDonald's after a two or three hour workout, you've just wasted time," McMillian said.

McMillian has given some of his co-workers and friends his diet and meal plan, and they reported 15-20 pound losses over a three month period. That bodes well for what he wants to do after he retires from the Air Force; become a personal trainer, helping people with weight problems and rehabilitating people with injuries.

McMillian is training for his last contest for the next two years. After the Junior Mr. America contest July 1, he will be giving his body some much needed rest. McMillian will PCS at the end of July to Bolling AFB, Washington, D.C. He plans on spending more time with his family and going back to school. He would like to become certified as an aerobics instructor, and is also highly interested in sports medicine.

McMillian said the two-year lay-off would be good for him and his family. He thinks Mary, his wife of 11 years, will enjoy the change.

"She's probably tired of eating chicken, turkey and salad without dressing," McMillian said.

McMillian plans on judging bodybuilding events over the next two years, and he said he enjoys gardening and writing poetry. Just because he won't be competing doesn't mean that people can stop worrying about him, though. He also loves playing intramural football and basketball.

"I've been told that I intimidate people a little bit out there," McMillian said innocently. "I've been told that I'm too physical, too, but if I'm running and I can't stop, sorry."

Dad winning Mr. Virginia Bodybuilding Contest to inspire me

God gave you one body and it is precious in his sight designed for his will and not for you to abuse with poor nutrition, smoking, drug abuse, alcohol abuse, and sexual promiscuity. Once your body is abused and used for inappropriate activity it will fail you and you will fail the God that designed it to glorify his purposes. Staying up late at parties normally will not have a pleasant outcome on your body and often time your well-being. Stay strong in all you do!

Emotional Fitness

This requires mental toughness and it is only conditioned by life's circumstances. When your life is filled with darkness, misfortunes, and a lost perspective, emotional fitness is a requisite to see it through and remain steadfast. Do not over-react to your feelings, but rather stand firm in your beliefs, fight the temptation to allow emotions to consume your mental capacity to eradicate the issue. Stay connected to optimism and believe it will get better if you invest the proper amount of effort and not surrender to a temporary setback.

Emotional fitness prepares you to recognize a problem for what it is without complicating the resolution, and render its emotional effects before it matures beyond your control. And if it is bigger than your ability to resolve, call someone you trust emphatically and loves you unconditionally. There are only three people I know you should call on, **1)** Your God first because he will never forsake you; **2)** call your parents, because we will always love you; **3)** call your spouse if you are married to a woman like your mother.

Mom and Dad at Christmas 2007; a joy to be your parents

Spiritual Fitness

The only methods to remain spiritually conditioned is constant study of your Bible, worship where you are spiritual feed to live, stay connected to God. Spiritual fitness will sustain you through anything and help you endure the burdens. God is always prepared to bless the sinner, the pure at heart and the righteous, even when we do not deserve it. He is knocking to get our attention, but we must be wise enough to hear the knock, spiritual enough to recognize the knock, and faithful enough to open the door and allow him to enter to bless our lives as he promised.

Troubles will find your address if you live long enough. There will be brokenness and you could find yourself in the pitfalls of hell. In such dire straits your spiritual fitness will pull you back to solid ground and give you a fresh roadmap, a new attitude, and no one can turn you around.

When I was a youngster, I was encouraged to lead a song in a local church youth choir. As you know I cannot carry a tune in a paper bag, but the lyrics of that song has remained with me all my life. The title was "Don't Let the Devil Ride." The lyrics were "if you let the devil ride he will want to drive and then he will turn you around."

Always allow your God to have the wheel when your life is in a state of flux, give him the wheel when you are looking for a miracle, give him the wheel when doors are closed in your face, give him the wheel when everyone tells you no, give him the wheel when your heart is broken, give him the wheel when contemplating sin, give him the wheel when you are about to quit or give up, and he will drive you through the storms and the sun will shine in your life again.

"But those who wait on the Lord shall renew their strength, they shall mount up with wings like eagles, they shall run and not be weary, they shall walk and not faint."

Isaiah 40:31

Lesson # 9

Words Matter—Choose Them Carefully

One of the things you will hear about your father is I'm direct with a no nonsense style and approach. That is true to a degree but one thing I had to understand that words once spoken you cannot retract them. And if you offend someone the only recourse left is to say I'm sorry. Saying I'm sorry does not provide instant relief to hurt feelings.

Some people are not conditioned for tough talk or tough love. That does not mean they do not need it but once you dish it, recognize you have implicitly committed to them your assistance as they mature. Find a style to deliver your message without losing the impact, be considerate of other people's feeling when appropriate but do not placate to their weakness, do not impose your will on other people but never compromise your beliefs because others disagree.

Someone coined the phrase, "think twice before you speak." I cannot over emphasize how profound these simple words are when you are dealing with people, especially in emotionally charged situations. I'm guilty of not thinking before I engaged my tongue and hurt your feelings. Therefore, it is critical to choose your words carefully when communicating with the people you love because all they will remember is the negative descriptions you used in the conversation.

Some of the lowest times in my life is when I allowed my emotions to dictate my response, and when it was over I could not take back my awful words or soothe the hurt feelings. There is a childhood rhyme that says "sticks and stones my break my bones, but words cannot hurt me." This is not true; words can leave scars of hurt. Respect the rights of others to express themselves unless they are condescending and disrespectful towards you. In those situations you have two choices: 1) respond in kind and make the situation worst, or 2) rise above the fray and remain dignified without demonstrating weakness. Quietness does not equate to weakness and "silence is golden."

Remember the old adage "God gave you two ears and one tongue" meaning twice as much listening and half as much talking. Dr. Martin Luther King Jr. suggested you can be either "justified or dignified" in your responses to negative situations. Finding the will to remain dignified is the most difficult choice when emotions are strong, but rely on your emotional fitness to keep you on the dignified sideline.

Lesson # 10
Resilient and Diligent

Resilience is the glue that will hold you in place when forces are moving everyone else in the wrong direction. Once you have established your focus, be diligent in the pursuit of your dreams; all is attainable. A man with a clear vision, coherent strategy and resilience to withstand the impacts of negative forces will reach their divine destiny.

Our African American ancestors are the best examples of resilience you will ever find in our history. Their examples must be the foundation for your toughness. African American ancestors were shackled, beaten and denied human liberties but kept the faith for you to never compromise your principles. Harriet Tubman risked her life to free slaves from the south to extend the life, liberty and happiness you enjoy today. The Tuskegee Airmen never gave up on their dream to inspire you to reach beyond the barriers to success. Dr. King marched, endured physical, mental and emotional brutality to compel you to die trying, rather than

stand for nothing. Rosa Parks sat down on the bus, tired and weary from a hard day's labor to ignite a change in the world for your future. The sit-ins were necessary to demonstrate resolve in our lives when the odds are not in our favor. Your father kept pushing through obstacles regardless of poor beginnings and no resources to illustrate faith and determination are winning combinations.

Resilience and diligence will equip you to summon the courage to stand face-to-face with adversities and dismantle them one by one. More importantly, it will force you to release the shackles designed to limit your possibilities. You owe your ancestors!

"The Sovereign Lord is my strength, he makes my feet like hind's feet and makes me walk upon high places."

Tuskegee Airmen, the Epitome of Resilience
Left to right you have Col. (Ret) Fitzroy "Buck" Newsum,
Lt Col. (Ret) Bob Ashby, and Capt. Samuel Hunter

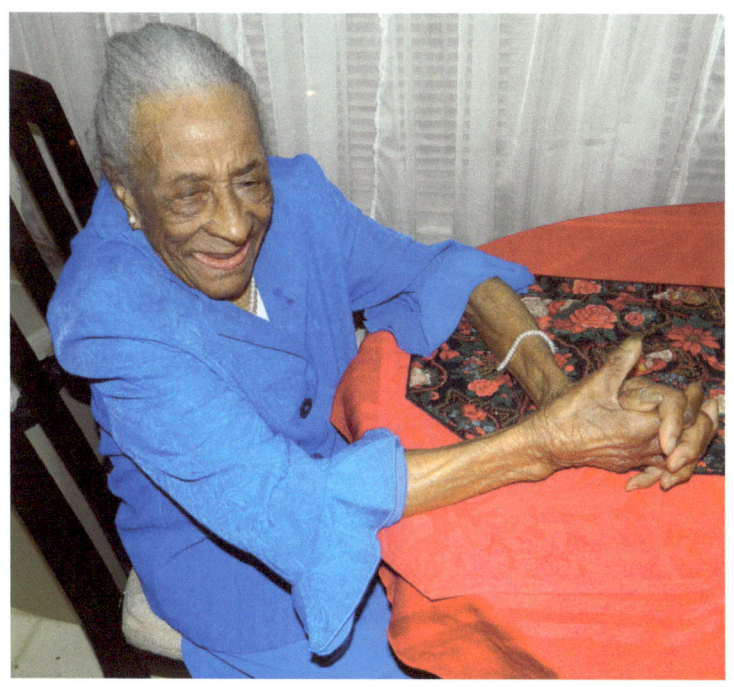
Great Grandmother Sophia at 103, perfect resiliency

"But select capable men from all the people, men who fear God, trustworthy men who hate dishonest gain and appoint them as officials over thousands, hundreds, fifties and tens."

Exodus 18:21

Lesson # 11

Hold Yourself Accountable and Be Reliable

"There is no excuses for excuses period." When a man fails to hold himself accountable for his actions and is not reliable, he loses his very soul. They break hearts, erode relationships in all its forms, they ruin organizations, mislead honest people, destroy families and strip themselves of character, courage and commitment. There will always be someone counting on you to deliver what you promised and if you fail them, you will never rekindle their respect. I promised you a dog since you were two years of age and I never fulfilled that promise. I could hear the disappointment in your voice and see the void in your heart through your bright eyes. It haunts me today for not meeting that obligation and I do not expect you to forgive me. I expect you not to make that mistake and live up to your commitments no matter how much it cost you. My excuses were not sufficient that compromised your happiness.

Accountability will be a cornerstone in your life forever and it will expose who you really are when you disassemble it. I do not want you to blame anyone for your failures, do not blame anyone for ignoring your opportunities, do not blame anyone for wasting time, or not being well prepared for any endeavor. The world owes you nothing and do not expect anything for free. You owe it to yourself to close the gaps that exist in your life.

Be the first to admit your mistakes, devise a solution and move on. Do not permit bad situations to hold you hostage because if you do, it will freeze you in time and put your life on pause. Once you start marching in place, the life you deserve is never realized and the disappointments years later will drain you until you die.

Self-improvement is denied when you do not hold yourself accountable. When you are not dependable people will not invite you in the circle of influence. Dependability is critical to developing sustainable value added relationships. There is little you can do in this world alone and having people in your court that trust you and respect you will elevate you beyond any measure of imagination. My career success is due, in large part to the trust my associates have had in my solid record of accountability and reliability. Therefore, they invested their valuable time and energy in my pursuit of success.

The accountability principle and consistent reliability will promote you to places only dreamed of by others. Whatever leadership position you aspire to occupy accountability will eliminate all doubt in the people you serve. During turbulent times your people will look to you for toughness and this is when unwavering reliability becomes paramount to plowing through the overwhelming fields of despair to preserve their faith in you.

Lesson # 12

Have Some Fun along the Way

Life without fun can be unassuming and dull. At the other extreme life with inappropriate fun can lead to permanent damage or worst death. I want you to enjoy your life without any regrets, and reward yourself for hard work but within reason. My definition of fun is to take vacations to places you enjoy, share special time with people you care about, keep your sense of humor to make people laugh. More importantly, learn to laugh at yourself as often as possible. Do not allow the stressors of your job or school rob you of a healthy outlook on life. Spend some time dancing it is great exercise and provides a temporary break from the daily grind.

I do not consider spending all night at a club inhaling everyone's smoke and pursuing irresponsible potentially life changing sexual encounters as fun. I do not believe binge drinking just to test your manhood or impress some fraternity is fun. And I do not believe participating in substance abuse to be accepted by the status quo is fun.

Fun is what you make it and you are responsible for the outcome, good or bad. Trust your instincts and design fun that is clean and right for you and your life. The best fun I have ever had was with you and your mother, or friends with common interest. Certainly, you recall some of the parties your mother and I hosted at our home for special friends, such as our Motown parties with the appropriate attire for the era.

Fun is to help you enjoy and appreciate your blessings, lift you from emotional drain, and feel good from head to toe. Add fun to your life and you will bring joy to others with your million dollar infectious smile.

"There are two ways of exerting one's strength; one is pushing down, and the other is pulling up."

Booker T. Washington

Conclusion

Son, I pray as you mature the words presented in this appreciation of you will be a small lamp light during your travels through life. I wanted to document the best lessons I learned in hopes that one day you will continue this legacy with your children. All fathers are charged with leaving a legacy to their children and too often we fail to meet that obligation.

I was not blessed with a father who cared enough to leave a memorable legacy for me, and I know the emptiness it can leave in one's heart. In these few short pages, I pour my heart in you, and when we are apart and our voices are silent, I want you to have these words to recall how much you mean to me. This is not where our story ends but the start of a great beginning. I will always be available to you for the rest of my life and you can count me to be there when you are at your worst and your best. I love you and I'm extremely proud of you.

"May the God of peace, who through the blood of eternal covenant brought back from the dead our Lord Jesus, the greatest shepherd of the sheep equip you with everything good for doing his will and may he work in you what is pleasing to him through Jesus Christ to whom be the glory forever and ever. Amen"

BRIGADIER GENERAL JIMMY E. MCMILLIAN
Retired   October 01, 2012

Brig. Gen. Jimmy E. McMillian is Director of Security Forces, Deputy Chief of Staff for Logistics, Installations and Mission Support, Headquarters U.S. Air Force, Washington, D.C. He is the focal point for ensuring the physical security of nuclear assets within the Air Force and planning and programming for more than 30,000 active-duty and Reserve components' security forces at locations worldwide. He provides policy and oversight for protecting Air Force resources from terrorism, criminal acts, sabotage and acts of war, and he ensures Security Forces are trained, equipped and ready to support contingency and exercise plans.

General McMillian earned his commission after graduating from the ROTC program at North Carolina Agriculture and Technical State University in 1981. During his career, he has served in a variety of security forces operations and instructor assignments in Montana, Texas, New Jersey, Nevada, North Dakota, Turkey and Washington, D.C. He has also served in major command headquarters positions at Air Combat Command, Air Mobility Command and Air Force Space Command. He has commanded at the squadron, group, and wing levels.

EDUCATION
1981 Bachelor's degree in business administration, North Carolina A&T State University, Greensboro
1985 Squadron Officer School, Maxwell Air Force Base, Ala.
1986 Advance Criminal Justice Course, Eastern Kentucky University, Richmond
1988 Master's degree in public administration, Central Michigan University, Mount Pleasant
1993 Air Command and Staff College, Maxwell AFB, Ala.
2001 Air War College, by correspondence and seminar
2003 Master of Science degree in strategic studies, Air University, Maxwell AFB, Ala.
2008 Executive Management Program, Pennsylvania State University, University Park
2009 Leadership Development Program, Center for Creative Leadership, Saint Petersburg, Fla.
2010 Enterprise Leadership Seminar, University of Virginia, Charlottesville
2011 Program for Senior Executives in National and International Security, John F. Kennedy School Of Government, Harvard University, Cambridge, Mass.

ASSIGNMENTS

1. May 1982 - July 1985, flight security officer and operations officer, 341st Missile Security Squadron, Malmstrom AFB, Mont.
2. October 1985 - September 1986, instructor and course chief, Air Force Security Police Academy, Camp Bullis, Texas
3. September 1986 - December 1989, training officer, Air Force Security Police Air Base Ground Defense School, Fort Dix, N.J.
4. December 1989 - February 1990, Security Police Chief, 7392nd Munitions Support Squadron, Eskisheir Air Base, Turkey
5. February 1990 - July 1993, Commander, 4554th Ground Combat Training Squadron, and Commander, 554th Security Police Squadron, Nellis AFB, Nev.
6. July 1993 - July 1995, staff action officer, Security Police Staff, and Chief, Inspector General Inspection Section, Headquarters Air Combat Command, Langley AFB, Va.
7. July 1995 - July 1997, Police Chief, Bolling AFB, D.C.
8. July 1997 - August 1998, Commander, 321st Security Forces Squadron, Grand Forks AFB, N.D.
9. August 1998 - November 2001, Division Chief, Security Forces Operations, Headquarters Air Mobility Command, Scott AFB, Ill.
10. November 2001 - June 2002, Deputy Commander, 99th Security Forces Group, Nellis AFB, Nev.
11. July 2002 - June 2003, student, Air War College, Maxwell AFB, Ala.
12. July 2003 - May 2005, Commander, 91st Security Forces Group, Minot AFB, N.D.
13. May 2005 - April 2006, executive officer to the Commander, Headquarters Air Force Space Command, Peterson AFB, Colo.
14. May 2006 - August 2009, Commander, 10th Air Base Wing, U.S. Air Force Academy, Colorado Springs, Colo.
15. August 2009 - present, Director of Security Forces, Deputy Chief of Staff for Logistics, Installations and Mission Support, Headquarters U.S. Air Force, Washington, D.C.

MAJOR AWARDS AND DECORATIONS

Distinguish Service Medal
Legion of Merit with oak leaf cluster
Meritorious Service Medal with silver and bronze oak leaf clusters
Air Force Commendation Medal with oak leaf cluster
Air Force Outstanding Unit Award with four oak leaf clusters
Air Force Organizational Excellence Award with oak leaf cluster
National Defense Service Medal with bronze star
Global War on Terrorism Service Medal
Navy Expert Pistol
Navy Expert Rifle

EFFECTIVE DATES OF PROMOTION

Second Lieutenant Dec. 18, 1981
First Lieutenant Dec. 15, 1983
Captain March 5, 1986
Major May 1, 1993
Lieutenant Colonel Jan. 1, 1998
Colonel May 1, 2003
Brigadier General June 19, 2009

A Psalm of David

The Lord is my shepherd;
I shall not want.

He makes me to lie down in green pastures;
He leads me beside the still waters.

He restores my soul;
He leads me in the paths of righteousness
For His name's sake.

Yea, though I walk through the valley of the shadow of death,
I will fear no evil;
For You are with me;
Your rod and Your staff, they comfort me.

You prepare a table before me in the presence of my enemies;
You anoint my head with oil;
My cup runs over.

Surely goodness and mercy shall follow me
All the days of my life;
And I will dwell[a] in the house of the Lord
Forever.

Psalm 23

www.ingramcontent.com/pod-product-compliance
Lightning Source LLC
Chambersburg PA
CBHW041401160426
42811CB00101B/1507